P9-CLS-531

THE LGBTQ+ GUIDE TO BEATING BULLYING™

Your Rights as an LGBTQ+ Teen

Barbra Penne and Patrick Renehan

Rosen
YA™

New York

Published in 2018 by The Rosen Publishing Group, Inc.
29 East 21st Street, New York, NY 10010

Copyright © 2018 by The Rosen Publishing Group, Inc.

First Edition

All rights reserved. No part of this book may be reproduced in any form without permission in writing from the publisher, except by a reviewer.

Library of Congress Cataloging-in-Publication Data

Names: Penne, Barbra, author. | Renehan, Patrick, author.
Title: Your rights as an LGBTQ+ teen / Barbra Penne and Patrick Renehan.
Description: New York, NY : Rosen Publishing Group, Inc., 2018 | Series: The LGBTQ+ guide to beating bullying | Includes bibliographical references and index. | Audience: Grades 7–12.
Identifiers: LCCN 2017006194 | ISBN 9781508174394 (library bound) | ISBN 9781508174370 (pbk.) | ISBN 9781508174387 (6 pack)
Subjects: LCSH: Sexual minority youth—Civil rights—United States—Juvenile literature. | Sexual minority youth—Legal status, laws, etc.—United States—Juvenile literature.
Classification: LCC HQ76.27.Y68 W66 2018 | DDC 306.760835—dc23
LC record available at https://lccn.loc.gov/2017006194

Manufactured in the United States of America

CONTENTS

INTRODUCTION

In today's world, teens who identify as LGBTQ+ often face more bullying, harassment, and barriers to success than their peers. LGBTQ+ is an acronym that stands for lesbian, gay, bisexual, transgender, and queer or questioning. The plus sign includes the many other sexual minorities or groups who share a common struggle for rights and recognition with the aforementioned groups. Although LGBTQ+ people generally live fully integrated into their surrounding communities, the

The LGBTQ+ community is an important part of our society, yet its members sometimes must march to have their basic rights recognized and protected. Here, members of the LGBTQ+ community participate in the New York City Pride March on June 26, 2016.

term "LGBTQ+ community" may be used to refer collectively to all people who identify as a sexual minority.

Unfortunately, there is a long history of discrimination against the LGBTQ+ community. This is because many people have narrow views on gender and sexuality. Such views generally treat heterosexuality (physical and sexual attraction to members of the opposite sex) as normal and homosexuality (physical and sexual attraction to members of the same sex) as unnatural. Likewise, some people believe that there are only two gender identities, male and female, and that a person's gender is determined at birth. In reality, many people don't identify with either of these two genders. There also those who do identify with one of those two genders, but it is the opposite gender of the one they were designated by their parents or doctor at birth. People usually try to justify such discriminatory views on the basis of traditional religious or cultural beliefs. However, mistreating or discriminating against another human being based on their identity is never okay. All human beings have a right to live safely and happily.

Because of the unique challenges they face, young LGBTQ+ people require special resources or protections to guarantee their safety and success. Like many other minority groups, special laws and social awareness are important tools to protect the LGBTQ+ community. As an LGBTQ+ teen, knowing about rights and having the resources to assert them is a great starting point for protecting oneself from bullying and discrimination.

So what are rights? Are humans born with rights? Or does the government grant them? Also, what rights do young LGBTQ+ people have? How does the law protect them? These are all great questions for LGBTQ+ youth to wonder about. Simply put, rights are the powers or privileges that a person may justly claim for themselves. All humans are born with basic human rights. Some of our most basic human rights are the right to life, the right to food, water, and clothes, and the right to an education.

Rights are one of the most important tools the LGBTQ+ community has to ensure its safety. Governments are responsible for protecting all citizens' rights. However, they do not always recognize or defend different groups' rights equally. By speaking out, protesting, and using legal means to defend or reclaim their rights, the LGBTQ+ community can ensure fair access to facilities and safe environments at home, school, and work.

Knowing and fighting for your rights as an LGBTQ+ person puts you in great company. Admirable figures such as Harvey Milk (the first openly gay elected official in the United States), actors Ellen DeGeneres and Laverne Cox, and activists Marsha P. Johnson and Sylvia Rivera (who were partially responsible for the 1969 Stonewall riots) are just some of the famous names who have championed LGBTQ+ rights and brought them to national attention. Their stories are distinct, but their goal shared: to fight for the recognition and protection of their community's rights.

UNDERSTANDING LGBTQ+ RIGHTS

What do you need in order to survive and thrive? Like any other young person, LGBTQ+ youth need clothing, food, and water. They need safe environments at home and at school. They need access to doctors and adequate medical care. They need loving relationships with family, friends, and romantic partners, and also fulfilling activities and hobbies. Perhaps most important, young LGBTQ+ people need freedom from physical or emotional harm.

Unfortunately, many young LGBTQ+ people see these needs go unmet. Teens in the LGBTQ+ community experience bullying, discrimination, and physical and emotional abuse at unacceptable levels in school, at home, in the workplace, and in their communities at large. Although difficult to track, various studies have reported that anywhere from 20 to 40 percent of homeless youth identify as LGBTQ+. LGBTQ+ teens are also disproportionately represented in the juvenile justice system, meaning they are arrested and sent to jail at higher rates than their non-LGBTQ+ peers.

What Are Rights?

A right is something that a person has a just claim to. They can be thought of as the powers or privileges to which an individual is entitled, or in other words, as rules about what a person has the

The LGBTQ+ community is diverse, as are its young people. However, one thing that all young people, LGBTQ+ or not, have in common are basic needs, including loving relationships and friendships.

ability or freedom to do. Rights may be social, ethical, or legal in nature. Some rights are considered natural rights. All human beings are born with these rights, regardless of their society's laws or customs. These include the right to life, the right to security, freedom from torture or cruelty, and freedom of religion and thought. Additional rights, known as legal rights, may also be given to citizens of a specific country. These rights may include the right to vote, the right to assemble, and the right to petition.

THE UNIVERSAL DECLARATION OF HUMAN RIGHTS

One of the best-known documents listing human rights is the United Nation's Universal Declaration of Human Rights. Ratified on December 10, 1948, the declaration's thirty articles establish a standard for the rights that every country should seek to recognize and protect for its citizens.

In theory, the countries that ratified the declaration acknowledge all the rights included therein as basic human rights. Nevertheless, the document is not legally binding for countries that have signed it. Therefore, it is important to understand that even though many of the rights activists discuss are widely recognized as basic human rights, not every country recognizes or enforces those rights for its own citizens. Still, groups seeking greater legal protections cite the

During its third assembly, the United Nations ratified the Universal Declaration of Human Rights. It has become the most important document listing human rights.

declaration often. Additionally, many countries that have drafted and ratified constitutions since the declaration was ratified have used the document as a model for the rights it protects.

Every year, the United Nations and international human rights groups celebrate December 10—the anniversary of the declaration's ratification—as Human Rights Day.

One of government's primary purposes is to defend and uphold the rights of its citizens. As such, many governments have constitutions or other legal documents that list its peoples' rights. The US Declaration of Independence is one such example. The early American document lists important natural rights, famously stating "…that all men are created equal, that they are endowed by their Creator with certain unalienable Rights, that among these are Life, Liberty and the pursuit of Happiness." The Bill of Rights also lists important rights that all US citizens have. Canada has a similar Bill of Rights, enacted into law in 1960.

However, governments do not always enforce all citizens' rights equally. Historically, minorities in the United States have engaged in long struggles to achieve equal rights. The women's suffrage movement of the nineteenth and twentieth centuries helped establish the right of women to vote. Similarly, African Americans have fought for equal rights since the time slavery was abolished. The civil rights movement of the 1950s and '60s was a moment of great success in establishing legislation to protect the equal rights of black Americans.

Who Is LGBTQ+?

Before the twentieth century, the LGBTQ+ community had little formal organization or representation in politics. In fact, many of the terms that make up the acronym LGBTQ+ did not yet exist. The ones that did exist didn't necessarily have the same meaning as they do today. Historically, minority groups have been more successful at demanding their rights when they organize as a community. Therefore, in order to understand how the LGBTQ+ community has and can continue to demand equal rights, it is important to understand the subgroups that form part of the community.

Over the years, terminology for various identities has changed. Many terms that were once acceptable or even embraced by subcultures in the LGBTQ+ community have become obsolete or considered offensive. Other terms that were once considered offensive now have been reclaimed by members of the community. The LGBTQ+ community is diverse, and different members of the community usually feel differently about terminology. It is always best to ask somebody which words they prefer to describe their own identity. It is also common to ask somebody the pronouns by which they prefer to be called.

"Gay" is a term most often used to describe homosexual men, or men who are mainly romantically attracted to other men. In the past, it was commonly used as a broader umbrella term for the entire LGBTQ+ community. Lesbians are women who are mainly romantically attracted to other women. People who identify as bisexual are romantically attracted to both men and

Many identities fall under the umbrella term LGBTQ+. Never assume somebody's identity. Ask them how they identify, as well as what terms and pronouns they prefer to use to describe themselves.

women. All three terms describe an individual's sexual orientation. Sexual orientation is a person's inclination in terms of their sexual attraction toward others or sexual behaviors. "Asexual" and "pansexual" are other terms that describe, respectively, people who do feel little or no sexual attraction toward others or people who are sexually attracted to others without regards to their gender.

While sexual orientation describes a person's attraction to others, gender identity is unrelated and describes a person's inner sense of gender. Somebody who identifies with the gender they were assigned at birth is known as cisgender. A transgender person is somebody who identifies with a gender other than the one they were assigned at birth. People who experience or express gender outside the male/female binary may prefer the terms "genderqueer," "gender nonconforming," or "genderfluid."

Despite popular misconceptions to the contrary, a person's gender does not have to do with biological markers such as hormones or genitalia. It also does not have to do with gender expression, or the clothing, hairstyles, and other grooming often associated by society with specific genders. Many people use gender expression to reinforce their gender identity, but others do not. How somebody dresses does not invalidate their identity.

"Intersex" is the preferred term for individuals born with genetic, hormonal, and physical features typically associated with both males and females. Intersex children are often forced by their parents to express one gender or another. They may be subjected to surgery as an infant as an attempt by their parents to make them conform to a specific gender identity.

Finally, the "Q" in LGBTQ+ can varyingly represent the terms "queer" or "questioning." Formerly considered an offensive slur, "queer" has been embraced by much of the LGBTQ+

community as an umbrella term for all sexual minorities. However, older members of the community may still find the term offensive. Always try to be respectful of others, and never use a term disparagingly. Of course, despite an abundance of terminology and identities, sexuality and gender is complex business. Many people simply don't know where they fall on the spectrum. "Questioning" describes anybody who may be examining their gender identity or sexual orientation. Avoid being dismissive of any friends who are questioning. Instead, support them as they determine who they are and what they need.

It is always important to remember that each different group or individual that makes up the LGBTQ+ community faces unique challenges. Furthermore, factors such as race and gender often make the discrimination faced by certain members of the community worse than it is for others. For example, a Latina lesbian woman may face homophobia, racism, and misogyny in her day-to-day life. Often, she must confront all three forms of discrimination at once. All members of the community must respect and support each other and understand their unique struggles. Although the LGBTQ+ community is diverse, organizing together in the fight for equal rights generally has been the most successful path to equal rights for its various subgroups.

CHAPTER TWO

THE HISTORY OF LGBTQ+ RIGHTS

The earliest wide scale organized attempts to assert the rights of the LGBTQ+ community came in the form of the homophile movement. The homophile movement formed in Europe and North America after World War II. It tried to counter misunderstandings and fear of the LGBTQ+ community (usually known at the time as the "gay community") by associating homosexuality with romantic relationships instead of sexual activity. It sought integration into and acceptance from mainstream society. Perhaps the earliest legal accomplishment of the LGBTQ+ rights movement was the Supreme Court decision in *One, Inc. v. Olesen* (1958). At that time, the court ruled that *ONE*, a homophile magazine, was not obscene and, therefore, could be legally distributed through the mail.

The Gay Liberation Movement

In the 1960s, LGBTQ+ groups began to organize on a larger scale and gain greater visibility. The various homophile groups of the prior decade merged into larger organizations invested in advancing LGBTQ+ rights. Prominent groups such as the East Coast Homophile Organizations (ECHO) and the North American Conference of Homophile Organizations (NACHO), founded in 1963 and 1966 respectively, formed at this time.

Prior to the LGBTQ+ rights movement, sodomy laws made sexual activity between members of the same sex illegal. People suspected of being LGBTQ+ were often fired from their places of work. Transgender women and drag queens (cisgender men who dress as women) were common targets of police brutality and raids. All too often, employment discrimination forced vulnerable members of the community to live in poverty and engage in sex work. Many community members were homeless.

SODOMY LAWS

Before the LGBTQ+ rights movement, the only laws explicitly governing same-sex sexual activity were sodomy laws. In the United States and Canada, sodomy laws were inherited from England. They outlawed a number of sexual activities for conservative religious reasons. These laws did not exclusively target homosexual sex practices. Rather, they outlawed any sexual activity that was not done for procreation (that is, intended to produce children). Such sex acts were also prohibited for heterosexual partners.

Until the 1960s, sodomy was a felony in every US state. In 1962, the state of Illinois removed consensual sodomy from its criminal code. This meant that if two adults both consented to such a sexual act, it would no longer be considered illegal. Gradually, many other states decriminalized sodomy. In 2003, a Supreme Court decision determined that sodomy laws were unconstitutional. In Canada, the Criminal Law Amendment Act decriminalized sodomy in 1969.

As early as 1959, a group of drag queens clashed with Los Angeles police at Cooper's Donuts, a popular hangout spot for the local LGBTQ+ community. Pickets and sit-ins became common forms of protests against police harassment and raids at LGBTQ+ bars, nightclubs, and other gathering spots. By the late 1960s, LGBTQ+ actions had become increasingly common in major US cities.

Another notable clash occurred in 1966 at the restaurant Compton's Cafeteria in the Tenderloin district of San Francisco. The cafeteria was a popular meeting place for trans and gender nonconforming people. Police often had used anti-cross-dressing laws as pretext to raid and shut down Compton's Cafeteria. However, in August 1966, one transgender woman resisted arrest, and a riot broke out. Although the incident received no media attention, it inspired many in the LGBTQ+ community to organize and form support groups.

The most famous clash (and one often cited as having started the gay liberation movement) was the Stonewall riots. The Stonewall Inn was a bar in New York City popular among drag queens, transgender patrons, and other members of the LGBTQ+ community. On June 28, 1969, a police raid of the Stonewall Inn prompted an uprising, as patrons rioted and clashed with police. Tensions in the neighborhood continued for several days, prompting the local LGBTQ+ community to form activist groups. Exactly one year later, the first pride marches happened in several major cities to commemorate the Stonewall riots. Pride gave visibility and momentum to many LGBTQ+ subcultures that had not sought to assimilate into society at large.

The Stonewall riots of June 1969 were one of the first notable clashes between LGBTQ+ protesters and the government. Police often raided the Stonewall Inn in New York City and unfairly targeted its LGBTQ+ patrons for arrest. The protests at Stonewall helped give rise to a cohesive LGBTQ+ rights movement.

Overcoming Legal Setbacks

Throughout the 1970s, the LGBTQ+ pride movement grew, but the HIV/AIDS crisis of the 1980s led to renewed social stigma and a backlash against the LGBTQ+ rights movement. The 1990s then brought a wave of legal setbacks designed to curtail the rights of LGBTQ+ citizens. Notably, US president Bill Clinton instituted the military's "Don't ask, don't tell" policy in 1994. "Don't ask, don't tell" prohibited LGBTQ+ people serving in the military from revealing their sexual orientation or gender identity, engaging in same-sex sexual activity, or being in a same-sex relationship. While a partial improvement on former policy (which directly prohibited LGBTQ+ people from serving in the military outright), the policy was highly discriminatory and unfair.

A discriminatory law called the Defense of Marriage Act (DOMA) was passed in 1996. DOMA stated that the federal government would recognize only marriages between one man and one woman. It also stated that states did not have to recognize same-sex marriages or unions granted in other states.

While the 1990s were a time of policy setbacks, LGBTQ+ rights advanced rapidly in the twenty-first century. Beginning in 2003, courts in several Canadian provinces and territories upheld the rights of same-sex couples to be married. This wave culminated in the 2005 passage of the Civil Marriage Act, which made same-sex marriage legal across all of Canada. In the United States, same-sex unions and marriages were made legal progressively in various states, beginning with Massachusetts in 2004. In 2013, the US Supreme Court ruled in *United States v. Windsor* that parts of DOMA were unconstitutional. This gave way to federal recognition of same-sex marriages. Then, in 2015, the court ruled in *Obergefell v. Hodges* that all states must allow same-sex marriages.

Marriage equality supporters rally outside the US Supreme Court as it hears a case on the constitutionality of same-sex marriage in June 2015.

Other laws passed under President Barack Obama further protected LGBTQ+ rights. These included the Matthew Shepard Act (2009), which classified crimes motivated by the victims' gender, sexual orientation, gender identity, or disability as hate crimes. In 2011, the "Don't ask, don't tell" military policy was ended. Various executive orders and rulings by the Equal Employment Opportunity Commission prohibited employment discrimination on the basis of sexual orientation and gender identity at the federal level (though at the state level and in private businesses, such discrimination is not always outlawed).

Where We Are Now

Since the wave of policies and laws passed under President Obama, the LGBTQ+ community in the United States has enjoyed greater rights and protections than ever before. However, certain rights are still not recognized by law, and some states have attempted to pass laws discriminating against specific subgroups of the LGBTQ+ community. Furthermore, some laws that protect adults may not necessarily protect minors.

In 2016, North Carolina passed a so-called bathroom bill, prohibiting transgender people from using bathrooms corresponding to their gender identity in public facilities, including public schools, libraries, and colleges. Legal challenges have been mounted against the North Carolina bill. Meanwhile, similar bills have been proposed in other states. In the same vein, some states, including Arkansas, Indiana, and Missouri, have passed "religious freedom bills," which allow businesses to discriminate against LGBTQ+ patrons on religious grounds. These laws impact LGBTQ+ teens, too.

Perhaps most damaging is the absence of laws protecting the identities and autonomy of LGBTQ+ teens with regards to their sexual orientation, gender identity, or intersex status. Though controversial and considered by most medical professionals to be pseudoscience, not all states explicitly ban "conversion therapy," that is, counseling efforts aimed at changing the sexual orientation of non-heterosexual teenagers. Furthermore, there are no laws establishing the legal rights of transgender or gender nonconforming teenagers to seek a gender transition.

Most of the LGBTQ+ community's greatest legal victories have been achieved in the courts. Photographed is Dana Zzyym, an intersex person who filed a lawsuit against the US State Department after being denied a passport for refusing to choose male or female as their gender. In November 2016, a judge ruled in Zzyym's favor.

In the intersex community, advocates are fighting to ban surgeries often performed on intersex infants to force adherence to either male or female biological expectations. Furthermore, gender nonconforming and intersex activists are seeking changes to government policies regarding gender listed on birth certificates, identifications cards, and other legal documents. They advocate for third-gender options.

CHAPTER THREE

YOUR RIGHTS ON CAMPUS AND ON THE JOB

Inside jokes at the lunch table. The jitters before a school dance. The relief of closing your locker on Friday afternoon. For most students, these experiences become their best memories of middle and high school. In hallways and classrooms, or maybe the locker room, gym, or school theater, students meet their closest friends and learn from their most influential mentors, developing what often become lifelong relationships, interests, and skills.

But for many students—and a disproportionate number of LGBTQ+ youth—experiences of harassment, violence, discrimination, discouragement, and isolation at school are just as common. In schools across North America, LGBTQ+ students face daily mistreatment by peers, teachers, and administrators alike, enduring greater levels of bullying and discipline than their straight, cisgender peers.

During their high school years, many young people might also start their first after-school or summer job. Everyone's first job should be a positive learning experience. However, work environments are another place where members of the LGBTQ+ community report high levels of discrimination and discouragement. All students have a right to an education and a safe school environment. Likewise, all employees have a right to work in a safe environment with equal opportunities to be hired or promoted, regardless of their sexual orientation or gender identity.

Your Rights at School

In the 2013 *National School Climate Survey*, GLSEN found that 74 percent of LGBTQ+ students reported experiences of harassment motivated by their sexual orientation or gender expression. Furthermore, LGBTQ+ students rarely see themselves sufficiently reflected in the content of their school libraries or courses. In many schools, they face difficulties forming student groups for themselves and allies, such as gay-straight alliances (GSAs). In the same 2013 GLSEN survey, more than 30 percent of

Asserting your rights starts with knowing your rights. Many LGBTQ+ teens and allies benefit from finding like-minded friends with whom they can discuss school policies or the problems they face.

students reported missing or avoiding school or after-school activities because they felt unsafe or uncomfortable.

As an LGBTQ+ student, knowing your rights is an important means of ensuring a safe, fair learning environment. All students have basic rights, and court decisions in the past have upheld students' rights. In the landmark case *Tinker v. Des Moines Independent Community School District* (1969), the Supreme Court ruling included the famous words, "It can hardly be argued that either students or teachers shed their constitutional rights to freedom of speech or expression at the schoolhouse gate."

On the national, state, and local levels, US and Canadian laws and policies define and protect the rights of LGBTQ+ youth in educational spaces. Again, these rights are most valuable when students know what they are and how to assert them.

Commentary, Clothes, and Clubs: Freedom of Expression and Association at School

All students have the rights to:
- discuss, voice, and display their opinions on LGBTQ+-related issues in speech, writing, or through other media, such as clothing;
- openly discuss their gender identity, gender expression, and sexual orientation;
- express their gender as they wish; and
- form LGBTQ+-related student organizations, including GSAs.

Any student in North America is likely to have heard of the right to free speech. Freedom of expression and freedom of association are constitutionally protected rights in both the United States and Canada. Expression is communication in any medium—whether it's an article in a student publication or a slogan on a T-shirt. "Association" means gathering together with other people for a common purpose, such as holding a meeting as a student club. While schools make many rules that affect the lives and learning of their students, they are required to respect these basic rights.

The rights of LGBTQ+ students, specifically, to express themselves and form groups are further protected by anti-discrimination laws and policies. Legally, LGBTQ+ students cannot be denied forms of expression or association that other students are permitted. Schools cannot require students to wear clothing based on a perception of their gender identity, for example. If a school allows some students to wear skirts, all students must be allowed to wear skirts. If a school allows some students to wear jeans, all students must be allowed to wear jeans.

Similarly, schools cannot treat LGBTQ+-related student groups differently from other student groups. If a school allows one extracurricular club to meet, such as a chess club, the school must also allow an LGBTQ+-related student club to meet. If the school doesn't require a parent's or guardian's consent to join the chess club, it cannot require such consent to join an LGBTQ+-related student club.

School officials can restrict these freedoms only in certain special circumstances. To restrict free speech, for instance, they

Students have the right to form LGBTQ+-associated clubs, such as GSAs, on campus. Such clubs can be excellent support groups and help change school policies to create safer environments.

must demonstrate that the speech in question causes a substantial disruption in the classroom. Schools sometimes use the possibility of disruption as an as an excuse to censor student speech, suggesting, for instance, that all discussions of LGBTQ+ issues are disruptive in the classroom. However, speech is not disruptive just because an administrator, a teacher, or another student doesn't like it. There are legal guidelines that define what disruption really is.

Bullying, Harassment, and Discrimination: The Rights to Safety and Equal Treatment

Unfortunately, having a legally protected right doesn't mean that a school or other students won't violate it. Along with the bullying and discrimination that LGBTQ+ students face as a whole, students also might confront barriers and abuses specific to their particular identities. For examples, same-sex couples may be refused entry to school dances or other school functions. Transgender students are frequently called by the wrong name and gender pronouns. In many schools, trans students are barred from using restrooms and locker rooms or from joining sports teams that match their gender. Gender nonconforming students may be singled out by teachers or peers for their hairstyles, clothing, or other elements of their gender expression. They may even be disciplined for their clothing, especially in schools with gendered dress codes. Intersex students find no acknowledgment of their anatomy in their biology or sexual education classes.

The right to safety and equal treatment before the law are basic human rights. Students who have experienced discrimination or harassment, or felt unsafe at school, should not feel alone—and they are not at fault. It is important to remember that discrimination and harassment are always wrong. No one should ever experience violence, ridicule, and exclusion, or receive an inferior education because of their actual or perceived identity, gender expression, or relationships. No matter who you are, what you look like, or who you date, you deserve safety, access to your basic needs, and the ability to participate fully in meaningful classes and activities.

The first step any student should take when they are facing harassment or discrimination at school is to seek out a trusted

DEFINING "HARASSMENT" AND "DISCRIMINATION"

Certain words carry special weight under the law. Understanding their legal definitions can be important in figuring out how to use certain laws to protect yourself and others.

Harassment is any unwanted and uninvited behavior that demeans, annoys, threatens, intimidates, alarms, or puts a person or group of people in fear for their safety. Harassing behavior includes, but is not limited to: degrading comments or slurs; unwanted sexual advances; nonconsensual touching; assault, such as pushing or shoving; or targeting a person or people with degrading public messages or images.

Discrimination is any unfair or unequal treatment of a person or group of people based on a defining characteristic, such as race, ethnicity, gender, religion, disability, or sexual orientation. Discrimination can take the form of a policy, such as the exclusion of LGBTQ+ couples from school dances. It can also take the form of an individual action, such as a teacher giving a lower grade to a student because of their gender identity, gender expression, or sexual orientation.

adult. This may be a favorite teacher. It may be a guidance counselor or school administrator. It may even be a librarian, coach, cafeteria worker, or janitor. Any adult employee of a school that a student trusts is a good first resource for protecting oneself from harm's way or reporting bullying or discrimination. School administrators must act to create a safe environment and discipline any bullying or teachers who are discriminating against LGBTQ+ students.

If complaints to teachers or school administrators fall on deaf ears, students have other recourses. Trusted family

One way of protecting your rights at school is by talking to trusted teachers, guidance counselors, or school administrators. Adults working at your school can help you enforce or change school policies for the better.

members such as parents, guardians, or older siblings may be able to help an LGBTQ+ student assert their rights. Students may also be able to contact their school board or district administrators if they are unsuccessful at addressing issues with school staff. As a final recourse, students may seek the help of legal organizations such as the American Civil Liberties Union (ACLU), who have better resources to make schools comply with the law.

Your Rights on the Job

LGBTQ+ youth also often face greater employment discrimination than their peers. To the disadvantage of some, workplace protections depend greatly on where one lives. Many states and localities prohibit discrimination based on sexual orientation, gender, or gender identity for government jobs, private sector jobs, or both. In 2012 and 2015, the Equal Employment Opportunity Commission issued interpretations of the Civil Rights Act of 1964 that prohibit discrimination on the basis of gender identity and sexual orientation, respectively. Executive orders issued by former US presidents Bill Clinton and Barack Obama protect all employees of the federal government from such discrimination.

Just as students do not lose their constitutional rights when they step onto campus, employees keep their constitutional rights while working. Policies that unfairly target LGBTQ+ employees and workplace harassment and discrimination are serious problems that must be addressed. As a young LGBTQ+ employee, similar steps to those that can be

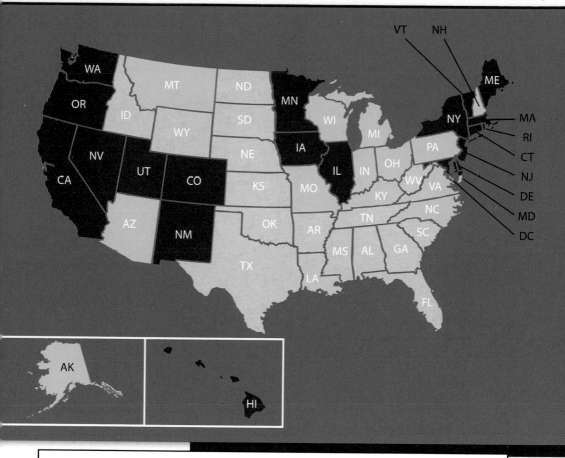

Protection from discrimination on the basis of sexual orientation and/or gender identity varies by state. Purple states on this map have laws protecting all employees from any such discrimination statewide. Blue states have varying degrees of protection from discrimination for employees and sometimes only for those who work in government. Gray states have no such protections from discrimination.

taken in school should be used to end workplace harassment or discrimination. Speak to a trusted supervisor or coworker. Reach out to somebody in your company's human resources department. If these options fail, rely on legal organizations that can help you assert your rights as an employee.

MYTHS AND FACTS

Myth: Students at every school have the same constitutional rights.

Fact: Constitutional rights apply only to students in public schools. Private schools, especially religious schools, are not required to respect the rights of their students, such as a freedom of speech or freedom of assembly, in the same way as public schools.

Myth: US law recognizes the right of transgender employees to wear work uniforms that correspond to their gender.

Fact: Title VII of the Civil Rights Act forbids employment discrimination on the basis of sex, among other qualities. However, court decisions have varied over the extent to which this same law protects transgender employees' right to wear work uniforms that match their gender identity.

Myth: The law and its interpretation by the courts are always just and always protect human rights.

Fact: While many people cite the law or court decisions when discussing discriminatory practices, in reality, there is a long history of laws failing to protect the rights of vulnerable minority populations. Keep in mind, in the past, forms of discrimination and abuse against racial minorities and women (including slavery) were often legal. We now know that those practices and the laws upholding them were wrong.

CHAPTER FOUR

BE WHO YOU ARE: THE RIGHTS TO IDENTITY AND PRIVACY

Every teen goes through a process of figuring out who they are. No matter their gender or sexual orientation, few teenagers start out feeling fully comfortable with who they are or how the world perceives them. In fact, discovering who you are and feeling confident about it may be a lifelong journey, and that's okay. You are not alone!

Sometimes, teens who identify as LGBTQ+ face extra hurdles in comfortably determining their identity and finding acceptance. In a youth survey titled "Growing Up LGBT in America," the Human Rights Campaign found a sharp distinction between the primary problems faced by LGBTQ+ and non-LGBTQ+ youth. Non-LGBTQ+ youth reported classes/exams/grades, college/career, and financial pressures as the three most significant problems they faced. However, LGBTQ+ youth's top three answers were families that didn't accept them, school/bullying problems, and fear of being out or open.

Article 22 of the Universal Declaration of Human Rights spells out the right to "the free development of [one's] personality." Every teen has a right to determine who they are and how they wish to present themselves to the world. They also have a right to privacy. This means they should be able to present their LGBTQ+ identity on their own terms and at their own pace.

Not all parents are readily accepting of their child's sexual orientation or gender identity. LGBTQ+ teens sometimes must educate their family about who they are and the right—and wrong—words to use when discussing their identities.

Coming Out: Your Right to Identity

"Coming out" is a term for revealing one's sexual minority status to others. Gender and sexual orientation exist on a broad spectrum. However, most parents and family members—even those who may end up being accepting, open, and inclusive toward their LGBTQ+ family members—tend to assume that children are heterosexual and cisgender. This assumption that being heterosexual and cisgender is the default often extends into social circles, as well. Until told otherwise, many people assume the identity of others. At some point in their life, LGBTQ+ people may choose to "come out of the closet," or outwardly affirm their identity to family and friends. The process of coming out can be hard, even if family and friends are accepting.

It may also require an LGBTQ+ person to educate their loved ones—both about who they are and what are their rights.

While everybody's "coming out" process is different, there are parts of coming out that most teens will encounter. Arguably, the most important part is becoming comfortable with one's own identity. Of course, identity is not fixed. It may change with time. Additionally, different people will feel differently about the terms they identify with. This is totally normal. But understanding different terms and identities will help every teen assert who they are to the world at large.

The right to a personal identity is a basic human right. Sadly, some family members, friends, coworkers, or others have prejudiced views toward LGBTQ+ people. They may try to deny an LGBTQ+ teen's identity. In some cases, this is a short-lived coping mechanism, and their

Alana McLaughlin, a trans woman, holds up a photo of herself from before her gender transition. Changes in gender expression can help transgender people affirm their identities to others.

CONVERSION THERAPY: WHAT IS IT AND WHY IS IT DANGEROUS?

Conversion therapy is a form of psychological counseling intended to force a lesbian, gay, or bisexual person (usually a teenager) to be heterosexual. It is not only controversial, but there is no scientific evidence to suggest that it works. In fact, LGBTQ+ rights organizations and psychiatric associations have challenged such practices as unethical, harmful, and pseudoscientific.

In 2000, the American Psychiatric Association reaffirmed that homosexuality is not a mental illness and, therefore, cannot and does not needs to be "cured." It also reaffirmed that no scientific evidence supports the possibility of changing somebody's sexual orientation. In 2009, the American Psychological Association issued the findings of a task force on conversion therapy. Its report stated, "… [E]fforts to change sexual orientation are unlikely to be successful and involve some risk of harm." The motivations for conversion therapy are usually conservative political or religious beliefs—not scientific ones.

In April 2015, US president Barack Obama called for an end to conversion therapy. Many US states and localities (including California, Illinois, New Jersey, New York, Oregon, and Vermont) have banned the practice for minors. It is also banned in the Canadian provinces of Ontario and Manitoba. Conversion therapy is a violation of an LGBTQ+ teen's right to personal identity. It also threatens their health and well-being.

denial of who their LGBTQ+ child, sibling, or friend is will turn into acceptance. While it is never a young LGBTQ+ person's responsibility, explaining their identity to loved ones and educating them about it often helps. Sometimes, loved ones may never truly accept an LGBTQ+ person's identity. The most important thing for every teen to remember is that only they can choose their own identity, and nobody else can deny or change it.

Against Being Outed: Your Right to Privacy

The process of coming out also involves deciding whom to tell and how. Coming out is very personal and should always happen at one's own pace. For some, it can be a gradual process that takes years. Others prefer to tell many people quickly. Coming out can happen over text or chat. It can be on the phone. It may be in person, or even through a letter or email. Every LGBTQ+ teen should come out in a way that is comfortable for them. The Trevor Project, an organization that provides support for LGBTQ+ teens, offers a free concise guide called *Coming Out as You*. The guide walks readers through every step of coming out on their own terms. It is available on their website (http://www .thetrevorproject.org/section/YOU).

Unfortunately, not everybody is able to control how their friends or family find out about their identity. Being "outed" is a term for when someone else chooses to reveal an LGBTQ+ person's identity without their consent. Being outed is wrong and very painful. It also violates a person's right to privacy.

The right to privacy is not explicitly written into the US Constitution. Nonetheless, the Supreme Court has upheld it as a right in several cases. Initially, two Supreme Court decisions

(*Griswold v. Connecticut* [1965] and *Whalen v. Roe* [1977]) defined and upheld a citizen's right to privacy. The court's decisions recognized two core principles of this right: the right to autonomy (that is, being able to make decisions for one's self) and the right to confidentiality (that is, secrecy).

The Supreme Court has not yet recognized an LGBTQ+ person's right to privacy in the context of sexual orientation, but some lower courts have. In *Sterling v. Borough of Minersville* (2000), a mother sued her Pennsylvania borough and its chief of police for threatening to disclose her son's sexual orientation, causing him to commit suicide. The Third Circuit Court of Appeals in Philadelphia ruled in the mother's favor. Its ruling stated, "It is difficult to imagine a more private matter than one's sexuality and a less likely probability that the government would have a legitimate interest in disclosure of sexual identity."

A 2007 California case also partially upheld an LGBTQ+ student's right to privacy with regards to her sexual orientation. In *Nguon v. Wolf*, a school principal revealed a lesbian student's sexual orientation to her mother while explaining a school suspension for having displayed affection with another female student on campus. The court ultimately ruled that the principal could reveal such information to a parent in order to explain the disciplinary action, but it also noted that if no misconduct had occurred (that is, if the student had not been violating the school's behavioral policies by publicly showing affection), the principal would have been violating the student's right to privacy in disclosing her sexual orientation. The right to privacy also extends to transgender students with regards to their gender identity or gender transition.

Charlene Nguon (*right*) stands with friends and family at a press conference. In 2007, Nguon filed a lawsuit after her school principal outed her to her mother. Nguon lost her case, but the decision did outline the general privacy rights of LGBTQ+ students.

The right to privacy is relevant to life online as well. A March 2010 CNET article cited an Iowa State University study, which found that 54 percent of young people had experienced cyberbullying related to their LGBTQ+ identity. Cyberbullying and forced outing has an extremely detrimental effect on the mental health of LGBTQ+ youth, and it constitutes harassment. Report any bullying, cyberbullying, or attempts to out you to a trusted adult. The organizations in this title's resources list can help you pursue justice.

10 GREAT QUESTIONS TO ASK A GUIDANCE COUNSELOR

1. If my friend or I have been bullied or called names by another student, to whom should I report it?

2. What should I do if a teacher is treating me or my LGBTQ+ friend unfairly and I think it's because of my identity?

3. Another student has outed me or my friend. Who should I tell?

4. How can I advocate for the inclusion of LGBTQ+ history in my history curriculum or LGBTQ+ writers in my English classes?

5. I am intersex and I don't feel properly represented in my science classes. How can I address this with my teachers?

6. Does our school have any gender-neutral bathrooms that students may use?

7. Can transgender students use bathrooms and the locker room that matches their gender identity? How does our school ensure their safety?

8. How can I encourage my teachers to call me by my chosen name and preferred pronouns?

9. My clothing is an important part of my gender expression. How should I respond to administrators and teachers who react negatively to the way I dress?

10. What should I do if an administrator refuses to let me attend a school dance with my same-sex partner?

CHAPTER FIVE

HOUSING, HEALTH, AND FOOD: YOUR RIGHT TO WELL-BEING

There are many ways that families and living spaces can look. Regardless of the form it takes, every human being deserves a safe and loving home environment. While many LGBTQ+ youth have caring families and housing, not all do. In some cases, families are supportive, but need information to best provide for a family member's needs. Other families simply do not support their LGBTQ+ relatives. They may dismiss their identity, obstruct access to basic needs (including medical care), or inflict emotional or physical abuse. They may issue ultimatums requiring youth to deny their identities or relationships. They even may throw them out of the house.

Article 25 of the Universal Declaration of Human Rights declares, "Everyone has the right to a standard of living adequate for the health and well-being of himself and of his family, including food, clothing, housing and medical care and necessary social services…" The right to well-being is a basic human right. Every person deserves housing, health, clothing, food, and medical care.

Recognizing Abuse at Home

Abuse is an unfortunately common occurrence for LGBTQ+ teens. Abuse at home, usually called domestic abuse or

Abuse can take many different forms, but it is never okay. If you are a victim of abuse, tell a trusted adult who can help ensure your safety.

domestic violence, may entail physical aggression, emotional or sexual abuse, physical or emotional neglect, or economic deprivation. Often, victims of abuse discount their own feelings and do not recognize the abuse they are suffering. Sometimes they are aware that they are experiencing abuse, but do not know how to stop it.

It is important to recognize abuse and know that it is wrong. Abuse by a parent, guardian, or older family member may take several forms. Such abuse often involves dismissing, mocking, or arguing about a teen's gender identity or sexual orientation. Sometimes, family members may insist an LGBTQ+ teen deny their identity or sexual orientation. This may take the form of forcing them to dress or present a certain way, especially for transgender and gender nonconforming teens. Unsupportive family members also might threaten to out a teen to other family members, neighbors, or friends.

For LGBTQ+ teens who require special medical care or therapy, restricting them from access to such treatment is another common form of abuse. Transgender or intersex teens, in particular, may require special medical care that other teenagers do not. LGBTQ+ teens in unsupportive households sometimes face punishment for owning LGBTQ+-themed books or movies, or for having other LGBTQ+ friends.

Abuse is always unacceptable. Family members may insist that abuse is justified, especially on conservative religious grounds. It is not only morally wrong to abuse another person, but it is also a violation of that person's human rights.

LGBTQ+ teens can and should seek help if they are ever being abused. This help may come from a supportive family member who also lives at home, such as an older sibling, and is in a better position to help improve living conditions. It may also be a relative, such as a grandparent, aunt, or uncle, who does not live at home but can offer help and housing, if needed. If a teen feels unsafe reporting abuse to another family member, other adults who may be able to help are a trusted neighbor, teacher, guidance counselor, or doctor. In extreme situations, it may be necessary to report the abuse to police.

The most important thing to remember is that housing, food, clothing, and medical care are rights, not luxuries. There are people invested in protecting LGBTQ+ youth's rights, including the aforementioned adults and legal organizations. Always report abuse.

Homelessness in the LGBTQ+ Community

Sadly, in extreme cases, parents or guardians will kick their LGBTQ+ children out of their homes. In some cases, a home environment becomes so unsafe that LGBTQ+ youth feel they must flee and become runaways. A 2012 report on the findings

A young adult uses one of the computers at the Ruth Ellis Center, an LGBTQ+ youth shelter in Detroit, Michigan. Homelessness rates are higher among LGBTQ+ youth than straight and cis youth, and LGBTQ+ teens may face greater risk of harm in many youth shelters that are not exclusively for LGBTQ+ youth.

of The Lesbian, Gay, Bisexual, and Transgender (LGBT) Homeless Youth Provider Survey found that nearly 40 percent of the clientele served by homeless youth organizations identified as LGBTQ+. The survey also found that the most common reason that LGBTQ+ youth became homeless was "family rejection on the basis of sexual orientation and gender identity" followed by young people who were "forced out of their family homes as a result of coming out as lesbian, gay, bisexual, or transgender." An astonishing number of homeless LGBTQ+ teens (32 percent) left home because of "physical, emotional, or sexual abuse."

Becoming homeless often exacerbates the problems a young LGBTQ+ person is facing. The National Gay and Lesbian Task Force Policy Institute's 2006 report on LGBTQ+ youth homelessness identified many of the biggest risks homeless sexual minority teens face. Among them were an increased vulnerability toward mental health issues, substance abuse, and risky sexual behavior. The survey noted that homeless LGBTQ+ youth are seven times more likely to be victims of crime than their non-LGBTQ+ counterparts, and they are disproportionately represented in the juvenile justice system.

Because of their increased risks, not all homeless youth shelters or transitional living programs are safe and secure environments for LGBTQ+ teens. However, specialized shelters and community centers dedicated to the needs of LGBTQ+ youth do exist. The LGBTQ+ legal organization Lambda Legal provides a listing of such centers in every state on its website (http://www.lambdalegal .org/publications/fs_resources-for-lgbtq-youth).

Access to Medical Care

Health care is a basic human right. Though political debates in the United States commonly center around affordable health care and whether or not it should be regulated by the government, all human beings deserve access to adequate medical care.

LGBTQ+ teens may have special medical needs. The Centers for Disease Control and Prevention (CDC) report that in 2014,

On World AIDS Day (December 1, 2016), local politicians and activists gathered for the unveiling of the New York City AIDS Memorial. HIV/AIDS is a health epidemic that has disproportionately affected the LGBTQ+ community.

gay and bisexual men accounted for eight out of ten new HIV diagnoses among youth. Furthermore, young people aged thirteen to twenty-four accounted for one-fifth of new HIV diagnoses that year.

THE HIV/AIDS CRISIS

In June 1981, the CDC reported the first cases of a rare lung infection affecting previously healthy young gay men in Los Angeles. After publishing its report, several more cases were reported of young LGBTQ+ people with compromised immune systems and rare illnesses, including an aggressive form of cancer called Kaposi's sarcoma. In late 1982, this disease was first named AIDS. By 1984, the National Cancer Institute had identified HIV, the virus that causes AIDS.

Throughout the 1980s, funding for AIDS research was often inadequate, and many criticized President Ronald Reagan for failing to quickly address the HIV/AIDS crisis. In 1986, the US Surgeon General Dr. C. Everett Koop issued a report calling for an education campaign, voluntary HIV testing, and increased use of condoms. These measures aimed to prevent the transmission of HIV. Still, treatment for those who were HIV positive was slow to come.

In 1987, an activist group called ACT UP formed to fight for faster approval of new drugs to treat HIV. In October 1988, the group led a protest at the Food and Drug Administration (FDA) headquarters. Just eight days later, the FDA greatly accelerated its approval process for new drugs.

Transgender youth also have special medical needs, especially those who are undergoing a gender transition. Though medical aspects of a gender transition, such as hormone-replacement therapy (HRT) or surgery, are not necessary to affirm a person's gender identity, for many trans youth, they are an important part of transitioning gender as they may help them more fully express their gender.

There are important tools to help LGBTQ+ youth stay safe and healthy. Proper usage of condoms can significantly reduce the risk of contracting HIV or a sexually transmitted infection (STI). Furthermore, the CDC recommends the use of preexposure pro-phylaxis (PrEP) for populations at a high risk of contracting HIV, including men who have sex with men. PrEP involves tak-ing a specified dose of specific HIV medicine daily in order to lower the chances of becoming infected with HIV. Its use can reduce the risk of HIV infection by over 90 percent.

LGBTQ+ youth with unsupportive families often face greater barriers to adequate medical care. Such teenagers may not have access to condoms or other HIV-prevention tools such as PrEP. These forms of prevention are important, given LGBTQ+ youth's statistically greater risk of infection. Transgender youth may not be able to get HRT or parental consent for medical procedures to help affirm their identity. Mental health services, which can help alleviate the effects of bullying, depression, or abuse for all LGBTQ+ teens, may also be difficult to access without parental support.

Another issue is that not all health-care professionals are sen-sitive to the needs of LGBTQ+ patients or fully informed on the best options for treatment. A 2009 survey of LGBTQ+ youth in the United States and Canada published in the *Journal of Adolescent Health* identified the need for greater sensitivity among doctors and health professionals. Research by the US Institute of Medicine found high percentage rates among medical students of discriminatory beliefs toward or discomfort with LGBTQ+ patients.

There are certain types of health care that all minors can access, regardless of parental consent. According to the New York

New tools exist in the fight against HIV, which disproportionately affects LGBTQ+ youth and young people of color. The US Food and Drug Administration approved the prescription drug Truvada for PrEP in 2012. Daily use of the pill by those who are HIV negative helps prevent them from contracting the virus.

Civil Liberties Union, these include reproductive health care, prenatal care, testing and treatment for HIV and other sexually transmitted infections (STIs), drug and alcohol abuse care, mental health care, post–sexual assault care, and emergency medical care. The CDC offers excellent resources for those seeking free and confidential health-care services. As a minor who may not

People celebrate the Supreme Court's decision defending same-sex marriage outside the Stonewall Inn, where the Stonewall Riots occurred in June 1969. In 2016, the site became a national monument.

have financial resources, discuss any necessary billing information and confidentiality with a health-care provider upfront. This will best ensure that your confidentiality is protected, if needed.

Looking Ahead

In many of his speeches, the famed civil rights leader Martin Luther King, Jr. stated, "The arc of the moral universe is long, but it bends towards justice." President Obama loved the quote so much, he had it sewn into a rug in the White House's Oval Office. The LGBTQ+ rights movement has come a long way, and undoubtedly, it has much progress to be made yet. However, arming yourself with the facts and understanding your rights is a powerful tool to assert who you are and what you need as an LGBTQ+ teen. If setbacks dismay you, recall King's words in your head. History is on your side. Always remember that a safe environment, equal treatment at school and work, access to medical care, and supportive relationships are not privileges. They are rights. By fighting for your rights, you are participating in a communal story and paving the way for a safer, healthier future for yourself and future members of the LGBTQ+ community.

GLOSSARY

AIDS Acquired immunodeficiency syndrome; a disease of the human immune system caused by HIV.

AUTONOMY The quality of self-directing independence.

CONSENSUAL Involving or made by agreement between the involved parties.

DISCRIMINATION Prejudiced or unfair treatment on the basis of a person's unchangeable qualities, such as race or gender.

HIV Human immunodeficiency virus; one of two viruses that infect and destroy helper T cells in the immune system.

INTERSEX A person born with genetic, hormonal, and physical features typically associated with both males and females.

LGBTQ+ An acronym that stands for lesbian, gay, bisexual, transgender, and queer/questioning. The plus sign covers other sexual minorities, including those who are intersex or asexual. Alternately, LGBT or LGBTQIA.

LGBTQ+ COMMUNITY A collective term for all people who identify as LGBTQ+, regardless of whether or not they live in the same place.

QUEER An umbrella term for sexual minorities; also used to describe non-normative sexual or gender identity politics.

RATIFY To formally approve a document, law, or treaty.

RIGHT Something that one may justly claim as theirs.

SEXUAL MINORITY Any group whose sexual identity, sexual orientation, or gender identity varies from the majority of society at large.

TRANSGENDER Describes an individual whose gender identity is inconsistent with the gender they were assigned at birth.

Lambda Legal
120 Wall Street, 19th Floor
New York, NY 10005
(212) 809-8585
Website: http://www.lambdalegal.org
Facebook/Twitter: @lambdalegal
Lambda Legal is the largest legal organization advocating for the
 fair treatment of the LGBTQ+ community under the law.

National Center for Transgender Equality (NCTE)
1400 16th Street NW, Suite 510
Washington, DC 20036
(202) 642-4542
Website: http://www.transequality.org
Facebook: @TransEqualityNow
Twitter: @TransEquality
The NCTE works to influence laws and policies, and end discrim-
 ination against the transgender community.

PFLAG
1828 L Street, NW, Suite 660
Washington, DC 20036
(202) 467-8180
Email: info@pflag.org
Website: https://www.pflag.org

331 Cooper Street, Suite 200
Ottawa, ON K2P 0G5

Canada
(888) 530-6777
Email: inquiries@pflagcanada.ca
Website: http://www.pflagcanada.ca
PFLAG provides support, education, and resources to the
    LGBTQ+ community and its allies.

Safe Schools Coalition
c/o Equal Rights Washington
PO Box 2388 Seattle, WA 98111
(206) 451-SAFE (7233)
Crisis Hotline: 1-877-SAFE-SAFE (1-877-723-3723)
Website: http://www.safeschoolscoalition.org
The Safe Schools Coalition works to make schools safer for
    LGBTQ+ students and teachers.

Sylvia Rivera Law Project (SRLP)
147 W 24th Street, 5th Floor
New York, NY 10011
(212) 337-8550
Website: http://srlp.org
The SRLP works to increase access to health-care, legal, and
    social services for people of color who are transgender, inter-
    sex, or gender nonconforming.

Transgender Defense and Legal Education Fund (TDLEF)
20 West 20th Street, Suite 705
New York, New York 10011

(646) 862-9396
Email: info@transgenderlegal.org
Website: http://tldef.org
The TDLEF offers legal services, public education, and community organizing on behalf of the transgender community.

The Trevor Project
PO Box 69232
West Hollywood, CA 90069
Crisis Hotline: (866) 488-7386
Email: info@thetrevorproject.org
Website: http://www.thetrevorproject.org
Facebook: @TheTrevorProject
Twitter: @TrevorProject
Tumblr: http://thetrevorproject.tumblr.com
The Trevor Project provides essential services for LGBTQ+ youth, including life-saving crisis prevention services.

Websites

Because of the changing nature of internet links, Rosen Publishing has developed an online list of websites related to the subject of this book. This site is updated regularly. Please use this link to access this list:

http://www.rosenlinks.com/LGBTQG/rights

Binaohan, B. *Decolonizing Trans/Gender 101*. Toronto, ON: Biyuti Publishing, 2014.

Bornstein, Kate. *Gender Outlaws: The Next Generation*. Berkeley, CA: Seal Press, 2010.

Bornstein, Kate. *My New Gender Workbook*. New York, NY: Routledge, 2013.

Boylan, Jennifer Finney. *She's Not There: A Life in Two Genders*. New York, NY: Broadway Press, 2013.

Coyote, Ivan, and Rae Spoon. *Gender Failure*. Vancouver, BC: Arsenal Pulp Press, 2014.

DeLine, Elliott. *I Know Very Well How I Got My Name*. N.P.: CreateSpace Independent Publishing Platform, 2013.

Erickson-Schroth, Laura. *Trans Bodies, Trans Selves: A Resource for the Transgender Community*. New York, NY: Oxford University Press, 2014.

Gino, Alex. *George*. New York, NY: Scholastic Press, 2015.

Howell, Ally Winter. *Transgender Persons and the Law*. Chicago, IL: American Bar Association, 2014.

King, Nia. *Queer and Trans Artists of Color: Stories of Some of Our Lives*. Createspace Independent Publishing Platform, 2014.

Kuklin, Susan. *Beyond Magenta: Transgender Teens Speak Out*. Somerville, MA: Candlewick Press, 2014.

Lam, Laura. *Pantomime*. Long Island City, NY: Strange Chemistry, 2013.

Lowry, Sassafras. *Roving Pack*. Brooklyn, NY: PoMo Freakshow Press, 2012.

Maroon, Everett. *The Unintentional Time Traveler*. Seattle, WA: Booktrope Editions, 2014.

Merbruja, Luna. *Trauma Queen.* Toronto, ON: Biyuti
    Publishing, 2013.
Mock, Janet. *Redefining Realness.* New York, NY: Atria Books, 2014.
Plett, Casey. *A Safe Girl to Love.* New York, NY: Topside Press, 2014.
Russo, Meredith. *If I Was Your Girl.* New York, NY: Flatiron
    Books, 2016.
Serano, Julia. *Excluded: Making Feminist and Queer Movements
    More Inclusive.* Berkeley, CA: Seal Press, 2013.
Sonnie, Amy. *Revolutionary Voices: A Multicultural Queer Youth
    Anthology.* Los Angeles, CA: Alyson Books, 2000.
Stanley, Eric A., and Nat Smith. *Captive Genders: Trans
    Embodiment and the Prison Industrial Complex.* Oakland, CA:
    AK Press, 2011.
Stryker, Susan. *Transgender History.* Berkeley, CA: Seal Press, 2008.
Taylor, Jami Kathleen. *Transgender Rights and Politics: Groups,
    Issue Framing, and Policy Adoption.* Ann Arbor, MI: University
    of Michigan Press, 2014.
Trevor Project, The. "Coming Out as You." Retrieved March 3,
    2017 (www.thetrevorproject.org/pages/the-guide).
The Universal Declaration of Human Rights. United Nations.
    Dec. 10, 1948 (http://www.un.org/en/universal-declaration
    -human-rights).

BIBLIOGRAPHY

Al Jazeera. "Obama Signs Edict Banning Discrimination Against Federal LGBT Employees." Al Jazeera America. July 21, 2014 (america.aljazeera.com/articles/2014/7/21/obama-signs-enda .html).

American Civil Liberties Union of Rhode Island. "'Students' Rights: School Dress Codes' Pamphlet." Retrieved February 12, 2017 (http://www.riaclu.org/know-your-rights/pamphlets/know-your -rights-school-dress-codes).

American Psychiatric Association. "Position Statement on Therapies Focused on Attempts to Change Sexual Orientation (Reparative or Conversion Therapies)." Retrieved March 2, 2017 (https:// psychiatry.org/File%20Library/About-APA/Organization- Documents-Policies/Policies/Position-2000-Therapies-Change -Sexual-Orientation.pdf).

American Psychological Association. "Report of the American Psychological Association Task Force on Appropriate Therapeutic Responses to Sexual Orientation." Retrieved March 2, 2017 (www.apa.org/pi/lgbt/resources/therapeutic-response.pdf).

BBC. "Obama Calls for End to 'Gay Conversion Therapies.'" April 9, 2015 (www.bbc.com/news/world-us-canada-32227353).

Carpenter, Dale. "Anti-Gay Discrimination Is Sex Discrimination, Says the EEOC." *Washington Post*. July 16, 2015 (https://www .washingtonpost.com/news/volokh-conspiracy/wp/2015/07/16 /anti-gay-discrimination-is-sex-discrimination-says-the-eeoc /?utm_term=.f9d06c1c4495).

Ettinghoff, Evan. "Outed At School: Student Privacy Rights And Preventing Unwanted Disclosures Of Sexual Orientation." Digital Commons at Loyola Marymount University and Loyola

Law School. October 27, 2014 (digitalcommons.lmu.edu/cgi /viewcontent.cgi?article=2888&context=llr).

Moffitt, Evan. "10 Years Before Stonewall, There Was the Cooper's Donuts Riot." *OUT*. May 31, 2015 (www.out.com/today-gay -history/2015/5/31/today-gay-history-10-years-stonewall-there -was-coopers-donuts-riot).

Moore, Elizabeth Armstrong. "Cyberbullying Hits LGBT Youth Especially Hard." CNET. March 9, 2010 (https://www.cnet .com/news/cyberbullying-hits-lgbt-youth-especially-hard).

National Center for Transgender Equality. "Know Your Rights: Schools." Retrieved February 12, 2017 (http://www .transequality.org/know-your-rights/schools).

New York Civil Liberties Union. "Private Schools and the Rights of Private School Students." Retrieved February 12, 2017 (http:// www.nyclu.org/milrec/privateschools).

Villareal, Daniel. "Before Stonewall, There Was The Cooper's Donuts And Compton's Cafeteria Riots." Queerty. Oct. 7, 2011 (https://www.queerty.com/before-stonewall-there-was-the -coopers-donuts-and-comptons-cafeteria-riots-20111007/2).

Volokh, Eugene. "Successful Religious Freedom Defense in Title VII Case Brought by Transgender Employee." *Washington Post*. Aug. 19, 2016 (https://www.washingtonpost.com/news/volokh -conspiracy/wp/2016/08/19/successful-religious-freedom -defense-in-title-vii-case-brought-by-transgender-employee /?utm_term=.ea5915826e8a).

INDEX

A

abuse, 43–45
American Civil Liberties Union (ACLU), 32, 52
asexuality, 13

B

bathroom, use of, 22, 42
birth certificates, 23
bullying, 4, 6, 8, 24, 29–31, 35, 41, 50

C

Centers for Disease Control and Prevention (CDC), 48–50, 52
cisgender, 14, 17, 24, 36
Civil Marriage Act, 20
Civil Rights Act of 1964, 32, 34
clothing, 8, 14, 26–27, 29, 42–43, 45
coming out, 36–38, 47
conversion therapy, 22, 38

D

Defense of Marriage Act (DOMA), 20
discrimination, 5–6, 8, 15, 17, 21, 24, 27, 29–34
"don't ask, don't tell," 20
drag queens, 17–18

F

free speech, 26–28, 34

G

gay-straight alliances (GSAs), 25
gender documentation, 23
genderfluid, 14
gender identity, 6, 14–15, 20–22, 24, 26–27, 29, 30, 32, 34–37, 40, 42, 44, 47, 50
gender nonconforming, 14, 18, 23, 29, 44
genderqueer, 14
GLSEN, 26
Griswold v. Connecticut, 40

H

harassment, 4, 18, 24, 29–33, 41
HIV/ AIDS, 19, 48, 49–52
homelessness, 8, 17, 46–47
homophobia, 15
hormone-replacement therapy (HRT), 50

I

intersex, 14, 22–23, 29, 42–45

L

Lambda Legal, 47

About the Author

Barbra Penne is an author living in Queens, New York, with her cat and two roommates. Her interests include literature, minority rights, and gardening. She has published nonfiction for young adults and children, including a collection of biographies titled *Transgender Role Models and Pioneers*.

Patrick Renehan is a queer, nonbinary transgender author and activist who lives in upstate New York.

Photo Credits

Cover, p. 1 Johner Images/Getty Images; pp. 4–5 Drew Angerer/Getty Images; p. 9 Rawpixel.com/Shutterstock.com; p. 10 AFP/Getty Images; p. 13 © iStockphoto.com/jeffbergen; p. 19 New York Daily News Archive/New York Daily News/Getty Images; p. 21 The Washington Post/Getty Images; pp. 23, 46 © AP Images; p. 25 shironosov/iStock/Thinkstock; p. 28 asiseeit/E+/Getty Images; p. 31 Monkey Business Images/Shutterstock.com; p. 33 Paul Stringer/Shutterstock.com; p. 36 JGI/Jamie Grill/Blend Images/Getty Images; p. 37 Barcroft Media/Getty Images; p. 41 Anne Cusack/Los Angeles Times/Getty Images; p. 44 djedzura/iStock/Thinkstock; pp. 48 Rex Features via AP Images; p. 51 Justin Sullivan/Getty Images; p. 52 Jewel Samad/AFP/Getty Images; interior pages background (hands) Rawpixel.com/Shutterstock.com.

Design: Nelson Sá; Layout: Nicole Russo-Duca; Editor: Jacob R. Steinberg; Photo Researcher: Karen Huang